THE THINGS THAT MATTER

Living a Life of Purpose
Until Christ Comes

DAVID JEREMIAH

W PUBLISHING GROUP™

www.wpublishinggroup.com

A Division of Thomas Nelson, Inc.
www.ThomasNelson.com

Unless otherwise noted, Scripture quotations are from *The New King James Version*. Copyright © 1979, 1980, 1982, Thomas Nelson, Inc. Other Scripture references are from the following sources: *The King James Version of the Bible* (KJV). *The Message: The New Testament in Contemporary English* (MSG). Copyright © 1993 by Eugene H. Peterson. Used by permission of NavPress Publishing Group. *New American Standard Bible* (NASB). Copyright © 1960, 1962, 1963, 1968, 1971, 1972, 1973, 1975, 1977 by the Lockman Foundation. *Holy Bible: New International Version* (NIV). Copyright © 1973, 1978, 1974 by International Bible Society. Used by permission of Zondervan Bible Publishers. *The Living Bible* (TLB), copyright © 1971 by Tyndale House Publishers, Inc. Wheaton, Illinois. Used by permission. *J. B. Phillips: The New Testament in Moden English*, Revised Edition (PHILLIPS), copyright © J. B. Phillips 1958, 1960, 1972. Used by permission of MacMillan Publishing Co., Inc.

Library of Congress Cataloging-in-Publication Data

Jeremiah, David.
The things that matter: living a life of purpose until Christ comes /
David Jeremiah.
p. cm.
Includes bibliographical references.
ISBN 0-8499-1794-8
1. Christian life—Baptist authors. 2. Second Advent. 3. Christian
life—Biblical teaching. 4. Second Advent—Biblical teaching. I. Title.
BV4509.5.J47   2003
248.4–dc21   2003007934

Printed in the United States of America
1 2 3 4 5 6 7 8 9 WOR 08 07 06 05 04 03

 *Contents*

Acknowledgments

First of all, at the center of my life is my wonderful Savior, who gives me life, energy, and motivation, whose written Word fills my mind and heart with thoughts that I cannot keep to myself.

My wife, Donna, knows my passion to communicate the Word of God, and during the long hours in which a book is being created, she not only understands, she cheers me on. This has been her consistent practice for the many years of our marriage. How blessed I am!

Our team at Shadow Mountain Community Church and at the Turning Point Ministries has also encouraged me. Glenda Parker, my administrative assistant at the church, served me in this capacity for many years and handled the myriads of details that could clutter up my mind and keep me from the uninterrupted periods of study that are the making of messages and books.

Carrie Mayer serves in a similar capacity at Turning Point. She keeps things organized in my office there, and her giftedness with the computer saves me hours of time both in preparation of the manuscript and coordination of its publication.

Sealy Yates, my personal friend and literary agent, wonderfully represents me to our publishers and faithfully represents them to me as well.

Finally I want to express my appreciation to the people at W Publishing Group for their continued confidence and trust. Thank you for praying for me and for working so hard to make *The Things That Matter* a project that will bring honor and glory to our Lord!

—DAVID JEREMIAH

Introduction

So many voices! We hear so many voices proclaiming what the future will bring. So many arguments. So many speculations. Everyone has a theory, an idea. And I'm not just talking about CNN, radio and TV talk shows, books and magazines, hundreds of websites, and *USA Today*. The voices predict everything from the greatest of manmade utopias to the worst apocalyptic nightmare.

Everyone, it seems, has a slant on what's to come and what we should be doing until it does. So how do you sort through all of this? How do you decide what to believe about the future? How do you identify the things that really matter?

I'd like to suggest there is one slant we ought to trust more than other slants, one "take" we ought to prefer above all other "takes," one opinion we ought to value more than all other opinions. Amid the thousands of shrill voices screaming for our attention and telling us what to do, there is but one voice we need to heed—the voice of the Lord Jesus Christ.

"But what does *He* have to say about the future?" you may ask. It may surprise you to discover how much He does have to say about the future. *Your* future. And it may surprise you to know what things He says really matter in the meantime.

Chapter 1
What Jesus Said about the Future

WHERE WERE YOU AT 11:58 P.M. on December 31, 1999? What was going through your mind? Was your heart beating just a little fast? Were your palms sweating? Were you concerned about what would happen in the next two minutes? Were you worried about the future?

That's a date that most of us will never forget. And when we look back on it now, we feel just a little silly about being so up tight, don't we? Our concern for the immediate future was wasted energy.

In stark contrast, the future didn't trouble Jesus, nor was He preoccupied with what might happen during His life on earth. Jesus knew what the future held, both for Him and for the world at large. As a result, we can confidently make four claims about Jesus' relationship to the future.

1

1. *Jesus Often Referred to the Future.* In Mark 13:23 He said: "But take heed; see, I have told you all things beforehand." Jesus was in the habit of preparing us for the future even during His days upon this earth. He made a point of telling those around Him some of the things they could anticipate in the days ahead. Jesus talked about the future a great deal.

2. *Jesus Rebuked People for Not Knowing About the Future.* Jesus also reprimanded and rebuked the people because they didn't seem to recognize that important prophesied events were taking place all around them. It was no small thing to Him that the people of His generation remained ignorant of God's prophetic Word. He expected them to open their eyes, look around, and put two and two together.

The Bible instructs us to *always* be looking for the day of Christ's return, not with wild-eyed speculations but with sober and Spirit-led discernment. We are to investigate what the Bible has to say and ask God to help us understand the day and the hour in which we live. We cannot remain ignorant of "the signs of the times" simply because thoughts of the future may make us uncomfortable.

3. Jesus Related Future Truth to Present Situations. The Lord used truth about the future to encourage and instruct His disciples about their present-day lives. For example, consider John 14:1–3: "Let not your heart be troubled; you believe in God, believe also in Me. In My Father's house are many mansions; it if were not so, I would have told you. I go to prepare a place for you. And if I go and prepare a place for you, I will come again and receive you to Myself; that where I am, there you may be also."

Here Jesus connected His ascension and return—both future events at the time He spoke these words—to His disciples' current experience of peace. He believed that by telling His followers what lay in their future, they would be strengthened to live more vibrantly in the present.

4. Jesus Revealed the Future So His Disciples Would Rest in Him. When you don't know how everything is going to work out, you have to hold tightly to the Lord God Himself and trust in the Lord Jesus Christ. We're told to "rest" in the Lord. That is the message we find throughout the New Testament.

So rather than spending all your time reading about the future and trying to figure the nuances of what it might hold, maybe you should spend at least as much time getting to know Him better. Then when the future becomes the present, you can be walking with the Lord Jesus Christ in strength. And you'll be doing the things that really matter.

HEAR HIS VOICE

My friend, if you do not know this One about whom we speak, this voice above all voices, the most important thing for you to do is to enter into a personal relationship with Him. It is not enough to go to church.

The real issue involves something quite different from that. The real issue is not singing hymns or doing volunteer work; it isn't even knowing the Bible. *It is knowing Jesus Christ.* Jesus is the One who said, "I have come that they may have life, and that they may have it more abundantly" (John 10:10).

Jesus gave His life for you, and if you will give Him your trust and do the things he says really matter, not only will He give you today, He will give you the future. You can walk into that future with His hand in yours, brimming with confidence and without fear, knowing that He is your refuge and your strength.

Chapter 2
Doing the Lord's Business Matters

ONE OF THE CRITICISMS often leveled at those who believe in the Rapture and imminent return of Jesus Christ is that such beliefs lead to a life of laziness and indolence.

After all, we *know* He is coming back. We know the end of the story. We've read the last chapter in the Book. Why should we entangle ourselves in the messy affairs of this passing world? Why should we soil our garments in the rough and tumble of the "culture wars" and the struggle for a more just and moral society? Why don't we just hold hands, sing songs, read psalms, and wait for the inevitable? What else matters anyway?

In direct contrast to that attitude, in a story told in the Book of Luke, Jesus used a phrase that keeps ringing in my ears. In my heart, I believe it ought to be the watchword for all believers who long for His coming: *"Do business till I come."* I love that.

Here is how that line fits into His story: "Therefore He said: 'A certain nobleman went into a far country to receive for himself a kingdom and to return. So he called ten of his servants, delivered to them ten minas, and said to them, "Do business till I come" ' " (Luke 19:12–13).

A similar story is told in the Gospel of Matthew. The latter parable dispels any notion of believers remaining idle while they wait for their Master's return. In this gripping story, Jesus gives us the key to our responsibilities as we wait for His coming:

> For the kingdom of heaven is like a man traveling to a far country, who called his own servants and delivered his goods to them. And to one he gave five talents, to another two, and to another one, to each according to his own ability; and immediately he went on a journey. (25:14–15)

Do you notice the similarity to the first story? What Jesus describes must have been a fairly common situation:

Then he who had received the five talents went and traded with them, and made another five talents. And likewise he who had received two gained two more also. But he who had received one went and dug in the ground, and hid his lord's money. After a long time the lord of those servants came and settled accounts with them. So he who had received five talents came and brought five other talents, saying, "Lord, you delivered to me five talents; look, I have gained five more talents besides them." His lord said to him, "Well done, good and faithful servant; you were faithful over a few things, I will make you ruler over many things. Enter into the joy of your lord." He also who had received two talents came and said, "Lord, you delivered to me two talents; look, I have gained two more talents besides them." His lord said to him, "Well done, good and faithful servant; you have been faithful over a few things, I will make you ruler over many things. Enter into the joy of your lord." Then he who had received the one talent came and said, "Lord, I knew you to be a hard man, reaping where you have not sown, and gathering where you have not scattered seed. And I was afraid, and went and hid your talent in the ground. Look, there you have what is yours." But his lord answered and said to him, "You wicked and lazy servant, you knew that I reap where I have not sown, and gather where I have not scattered seed. So you ought to have deposited my money with the bankers, and at my coming I would have received back my own with interest. So take the talent from him, and give it to him who has ten talents. For to everyone who has, more will be given, and he will have abundance; but from him who does not have, even what he has will be taken away. And cast the unprofitable servant into the outer darkness. There will be weeping and gnashing of teeth." (Matthew 25:14–30).

The earlier story underlines the importance of waiting for the Lord and always watching for His return. But the parable of the talents teaches us what to do *while* we are waiting. The bottom line? We need to be *working.* We're not to be sitting around drinking diet soda and playing *Bible Monopoly.* We're to be involved, energized, doing business for our Lord.

The parable of the talents warns us against laziness and passivity in our outward vocations. It warns us to keep our hearts with all diligence. While the first parable emphasizes attitude, the second emphasizes action. Both parables encourage us to watch for His appearing and to faithfully labor in the work of God while we wait for that great day.

The point of the "talents" story is to show us what we're to be about while we anticipate and look forward to our Lord's return. First of all, notice . . .

THE UNCERTAIN RETURN

"A man traveling to a far country . . . called his own servants and delivered his goods to them" (Matthew 25:14).

In those days, long business journeys were inevitable. There were no airplanes, no trains, taxicabs, or rental cars. As a result, a business trip to another nation or distant city might mean weeks of travel. But what would the householder or business owner do about matters at home while he was gone? Commonly, he would give over responsibilities of his estate to trusted servants. Those servants were charged with handling affairs while the master pursued business elsewhere.

When the lord of the household said, "I'm going to a far country," he had no idea when he would return—nor did his servants. Yet he expected those servants to be ready for his return every day. What a powerful reminder that you and I are called to serve Jesus Christ in His absence, always looking for His return, even though we don't know when it will be!

Our Lord does expect us to watch for His return; yet as we watch, we are to keep working in His behalf.

THE UNEQUAL RESPONSIBILITIES

Notice next that as he discharged the responsibility for the estate in his absence, he gave his servants some unequal responsibilities: "And to one he gave five talents, to another two, and to another one, to each according to his own ability; and immediately he went on a journey" (Matthew 25:15).

The *talents* spoken of here are not spiritual gifts or

abilities, as the word implies in our culture today. A talent was simply a measure of money—a monetary term. (But we wouldn't be off the mark to apply the principle here to our gifts and abilities.)

So he gave one man five talents, another man two, and a third man just one. Please notice . . .

1. *The Talents Were Dispensed According to the Judgment of the Lord.* Why did the master in that story give differing amounts as he did? Jesus does not offer a reason. He simply did it because he was who he was. In the same way, God does what He does because He is Who He is. Who's going to question Him? Who's going to ask Him, "Why have You done this or that?"

Whenever God gives us an endowment or a responsibility, it is always according to His own judgment, His own determination. My friend, that thought ought to fill you with praise and adoration for almighty God for *whatever* you might have. Because whatever you've got, it's from His hand.

Romans 12:6 speaks of our having "gifts differing according to the grace that is given to us." God gives according to His own judgment, and His judgments are right. Notice a second truth about that dispersal.

2. *The Talents Were Dispensed According to the Capacity of the Steward.* The Bible tells us the talents were given "to each according to his own ability." The fact is, God knows who we are and what we can handle.

Do you remember the business concept that surfaced some years ago called "the Peter principle?" The original wording by the author, L. Peter, went like this: "In a hierarchy, every employee tends to rise to his level of incompetence."[1] In other words, people tend to get promoted beyond their capabilities. They start off knowing what they're doing and have a good handle on their tasks. By the time they're through being promoted, however, they're in way over their heads! God doesn't do that. He never promotes anybody beyond his or her capacity.

3. *The Talents Were Dispensed in Order to Fully Equip Each Man.* The five-talent person wasn't any more "complete" than the two-talent man or the one-talent man. Whatever we have from God— if He gave it to us and He knows it to be perfect and appropriate for us—we are complete in that gifting. Just as the master left his servants in charge of various portions of his estate, so God has given every one of us what we need to accomplish His purpose for our lives. We all have what God knows we need!

Now you've got the picture. The landowner went away and gave his three servants some specific things to administrate. He rode off down the road on his donkey and disappeared into the distance. Now . . . what must those servants do? They must discipline themselves to continue acting and doing business just as if the master were still with them.

It isn't easy to stay accountable when the boss isn't looking over your shoulder, is it? It isn't easy to keep the routine when you don't have to get up at a specific time or punch a time clock. In this case, the boss couldn't check in by cell phone, palm pilot text messaging, or e-mail. The servants are simply left to do their work; he has to trust them to act in his best interest. As usual, two servants responded one way, and one responded in another way.

1. *The Faithful Men Doubled Their Endowments.* "Then he who had received the five talents went and traded with them, and made another five talents" (Matthew 25:16). Not bad! That's a 100 percent increase. That's "doing business," isn't it?

"And likewise he who had received two gained two more also" (v. 17). He also doubled the master's money. That's good investment, good stewardship.

Which of them did better? Actually, they did the same. They took what they had and increased it in the identical proportion. Which one had more? The one who had five—but he also had more to start with. Who had less? The one who had two—but he had less to start with. He took what he had, improved it, and made it something better than it was.

2. The Unfaithful Man Hoarded His Endowment.
"But he who had received one went and dug in the ground, and hid his lord's money" (v. 18). This last employee didn't do anything with his endowment. He was so afraid of losing it, he probably took his shovel out to the corner of the estate in the dead of night and buried that solitary talent.

I can just see this old Fearful Charlie. Every morning when he was out walking the dog, he walked by that place where the money was buried—just to make sure it hadn't been disturbed. *Still safe and sound!* he told himself. *Boy oh boy, the boss is going to be so proud of me! I didn't spend one nickel of what he gave me. Put it all in the ground and covered it all up. When he gets back, I'm going to dig it up and hand it to him as he walks through the gate. He's going to be so happy.*

THE UNIQUE REWARD

The lord said to the faithful men, "Well done, good and faithful servant; you were faithful over a few things, I will make you ruler over many things. Enter into the joy of your lord" (Matthew 25:21, 23). There was a *commendation*, a *promotion*, and an *invitation*.

The two servants who had doubled their master's money were called before him. He commended them for doing business while he was away—for taking their initial investments and multiplying them. As a result, each received a significant promotion. "Well done, good and faithful servant. I have given you a little to manage. Now you are going to have much to manage."

Has the thought ever gripped you, my friend, that the way you pursue the Lord's business in this world today determines the kind of administration you will have in the coming kingdom? Do you ever ponder that? The way you exercise your responsibility *now* will have a direct impact on what responsibility you will be given *then.*

So, my friend, if you want to have more—in this life or the next—you had better manage what He has already given you as faithfully as you possibly can. The people God trusts with more are those who have proven faithful with little.

THE UNTHINKABLE REBUKE

You may find yourself identifying a bit with the fear expressed by the one-talent man: "I knew you to be a hard man, reaping where you have not sown, and gathering where you have not scattered seed. And I was afraid" (Matthew 25:24).

This man failed because he did not know and, therefore, did not trust his master. But his lord answered and said to him, "You wicked and lazy servant, you knew that I reap where I have not sown, and gather where I have not scattered seed. So you ought to have deposited my money with the bankers, and at my coming I would have received back my own with interest. So take the talent from him, and give it to him who has ten talents." (vv. 26–28)

The result of his failure? He was condemned. And why was he condemned? The point was not that he had done something wrong. The point was that *he hadn't done anything.*

That's where so many of God's people find themselves in the kingdom today. It's not that they're doing bad things and undercutting the work of God. It is just that they're not doing much of anything at all. But, friends, this is not a time to sit on our hands. This is a time for us to get busy for almighty God as never before! This is a time for using every gift and ability He has so graciously given us to advance His Word and His will in our world.

"Well," you say, "that's easy for you. You're a preacher and an author. You know what you're supposed to be doing. But I don't know what I'm supposed to be doing."

My reply would be, "What has God put into your hand? What has He given you? What are your opportunities?" If you are a Christian, you (yes, you!) have a special gifting from God the Holy Spirit. Those gifts usually follow along lines you can identify in your own life. You may have the gift of helping. Or the gift of mercy. Or the gift of teaching and exhortation. Or the gift of administration. God gave me the gift of teaching, and I do everything I can to multiply that gift, to manage that gift, and to use it with all of my heart. If I don't do those things, I am an unfaithful, unprofitable servant, and the Lord will call me to account for that someday.

Whatever God has gifted you to do, my friend, do it! Manage that gift, make it work, grow it, develop it, practice it, and in God's wonderful grace, make it multiply. What God has given to you as an ability, give back to Him as an improved ability by managing it with all of your heart. That is what this parable is all about.

WHERE TO START

You say, "All right, Jeremiah, specifically, what am I supposed to do?" Are you wondering where to dip your oar into the Lord's work? Let me use the rest of this book to give you some places to launch. If you're doing these things in the power of the Spirit, you cannot—I repeat, *cannot*—go wrong. And I firmly believe that as you plunge into the Lord's work, He will direct and guide you more specifically into unique areas of service for His name and His glory.

Believing in the imminent return of Jesus is not simply a matter of "waiting," as important as that may be. It is rather a matter of *working*. Working hard. Working faithfully. Working in the power and joy and filling of the Holy Spirit. And when you work in such a way, you never know what God may be up to! You never know where your next kingdom assignment might be.

Someone asked me what I would like to be doing when the Lord comes back. That's easy. I would like to be standing behind my pulpit before my flock, declaring and explaining and applying the Word of God. For me, there's nothing better. There is no greater joy.

What would you like to be doing when He returns? Where would you like to be when the trumpet sounds, when the archangel shouts, and when in the twinkling of an eye we are changed and race into the clouds to meet Him?

What has He given you to do?

Do that.

Do the Lord's business until He comes. That's what matters most.

Chapter 3
Evangelizing Matters

LAST WORDS OUGHT TO BE LISTENED TO. People often save their most important instructions, their most profound thoughts, their deepest concerns, and their most heartfelt expressions for last.

Pancho Villa, the infamous Mexican bandit, must have realized that as he lay dying. Bidding one of his compatriots to draw near, he whispered into the man's ear, "Tell them I said something!" And then he died. True story! The man had the right idea—he just didn't have anything to say.

Oscar Wilde, the celebrated Irish playwright whose wit and debauched lifestyle eventually brought him to ruin, was taking a last sip from a borrowed bottle of champagne. "I am dying as I've lived; beyond my means," he announced. Then, glancing around the room, the penniless and disgraced writer quipped, "This wallpaper is killing me; one of us has got to go."[1]

He went.

Many times, however, the last words a man or woman speaks before stepping into eternity can be extremely significant. Sometimes a dying individual may catch a glimpse of what lays ahead, either the glories of heaven or the terrors of hell.

The Holy Spirit recorded the last words of Jesus before He left this earth. And as we might expect, those words are deeply significant. In both the Gospel of Matthew and the Book of Acts, we read our Lord's departing instructions to His disciples—and to all who follow Him—before He was taken up from sight.

Think of it! We have a written record of the very last words the Son of God uttered before ascending to the right hand of His Father in heaven. And these are the words—perhaps more than any others—that Jesus wanted to echo in His disciples' ears as He left them and until He returned.

He didn't say: "Organize a political action committee" or "Remember to work for justice and visualize world peace."

He didn't say: "Be tolerant of one another," "Save the whales," "Celebrate diversity," or "Commit random acts of kindness."

What He *did* say was as clear as bright sunlight on a cloudless morning. There was nothing obscure or hazy about His final instructions: "You shall receive power when the Holy Spirit has come upon you; and you shall be witnesses to Me in Jerusalem, and in all Judea and Samaria, and to the end of the earth" (Acts 1:8).

These words echo the Great Commission given by Christ in Matthew 28: "All authority has been given to Me in heaven and on earth. Go therefore and make disciples of all the nations, baptizing them in the name of the Father and of the Son and of the Holy Spirit, teaching them to observe all things that I have commanded you; and lo, I am with you always, even to the end of the age" (vv. 18–20).

WHAT TO DO?

Is it really all that difficult for you and me to figure out what the Lord wants us to do while we wait for

His return? Is it rocket science? Is it truly so puzzling and confusing?

Actually, it couldn't be simpler. As you study the Bible, it's interesting to note that these words are not only His final emphasis; He emphasized them from the very dawn of His ministry.

In Matthew 4:19, He said, "Follow Me, and I will make you fishers of men."

In Luke 19:10, He told Zacchaeus and the crowds: "For the Son of Man has come to seek and to save that which was lost."

As Jesus gave His great message on the bread of life in John 6, He declared that He had come down from heaven not to do His own will, but the will of the One who sent Him. And then He added: "And this is the will of him who sent me, that I shall lose none of all that he has given me, but raise them up at the last day" (John 6:39 NIV).

Anyone who listens even casually to the words of the Lord Jesus quickly catches up with the passion of His heart. That is why we must be very careful about allowing end-time concerns to distract us from the great passion of our Lord's heart. Remember what

Jesus said to the disciples in Acts? "It is not for you to know times or seasons which the Father has put in His own authority" (1:7).

I love to follow world news and keep my eyes wide open for signs of His coming. But, my friend, we can become so caught up in these prophetic issues that we walk right by people who don't know Jesus Christ.

What do you think the Lord Jesus would say about date-setting and dire predictions if He were to stand behind the pulpit in your church this Sunday? What would He have said about the madness that the world would end in the year 2000? I think He would repeat what He said at both the beginning and the close of His ministry. I think He would repeat the last words He uttered before He returned to heaven: "Go into all the world and take the message of salvation to every man, woman, and child. I'm counting on you to spread the word."

THE LIFE JESUS LIVED

Our Lord made evident His deep concern for the lost not only by the way He spoke, but also by the way He lived. Encounters with people punctuated our Lord's earthly walk. Public and private. Men and women. Children and grandparents. Rich and poor. High and low. Esteemed and despised. Religious leaders and prostitutes. Soldiers and tax collectors. Priests and pagans. For three years Jesus wrote the book on personal evangelism. All of these encounters testified to His supreme desire to win and to save those who did not yet know Him.

When the time came for Jesus to select the men who would follow Him and carry on His ministry, the Scripture says He carefully chose men who would *do what He did*. From the very first day that each disciple began to follow Jesus Christ, he knew what he would be doing. He was called to be a fisher of men. He was called to be an evangelist to tell others about Messiah Jesus.

Andrew got the idea right away. Scripture records that one of the first two men to follow Jesus "was Andrew, Simon Peter's brother. He first found his own brother Simon, and said to him, 'We have found the Messiah' (which is translated, the Christ). And he brought him to Jesus" (John 1:40–42).

In the words of Jesus, in the life of Jesus, and in the men He selected to follow Him, the thing that mattered most to Him was evangelizing.

TIME TO TAKE STOCK

What should we be thinking about as we move through the first decade of a new century? What thoughts should occupy our minds? Sometimes I think we just need to reread the directions and go back to the simplicity of what Jesus told us to do. Maybe we've strayed off course a bit. Maybe we've become a little too sophisticated for our own good. Maybe we've forgotten that the primary plan in the heart of Jesus when He instructed His disciples is *still* the primary plan. And if we don't go back and review that, if we don't let the Lord's words penetrate our hearts afresh, we might find ourselves chasing rabbit trails.

The disciples certainly got the idea after Jesus ascended. It took a little angelic nudge to get them jump-started, but after that they followed the Lord's specific instructions and returned to Jerusalem.

They had been told to wait until they were clothed with power from on high.

After Pentecost, after the Holy Spirit came upon them in power, they went out to follow the orders of their ascended Commander in Chief. In just a few short years they fulfilled the promise of Christ that they would do greater things than even He had done. Starting with a handful of men and women on the Day of Pentecost, that little ragtag band of disciples grew and multiplied until at the end of seven years, their number totaled at least a hundred thousand souls — and possibly many more than that.

No wonder the apostles were accused of "turning the world upside down"! The religious leaders of the day complained that these disciples had "filled Jerusalem" with Christ's doctrine. People were saying, "You can't go anywhere without running into this talk about Jesus."

Why did that happen? Because everywhere these new believers went they shared the story of Jesus, who had so transformed their own hearts.

THE CHURCH JESUS FOUNDED

What did the early church have that today's church doesn't have?

We have so much more sophistication: big screens, television, radio networks, websites, tape ministries, beautiful facilities, trained workers, professional instruments, and on and on it goes. We have resources. We have tools. We have education. We have prosperity and comfort and safety. But do you know what that first-century church had? *It had one throbbing heartbeat of purpose.*

In his letter to the Romans, Paul wrote, "I thank my God through Jesus Christ for you all, that your faith is spoken of throughout the whole world" (Romans 1:8). In other words, "Everywhere you Roman believers go, people know who you are. The message of your faith in Christ has gone out ahead of you."

The apostle had a similar commendation for the believers at Thessalonica: "You became imitators of us and of the Lord; in spite of severe suffering, you welcomed the message with the joy given by the Holy Spirit. And so you became a model to all the believers in Macedonia and Achaia. The Lord's message rang out from you not only in Macedonia and Achaia—your faith in God has become known everywhere" (1 Thessalonians 1:6–8 NIV).

Paul said, in effect, "We came here to Thessalonica to evangelize, but because of you, the message is already out there. Everybody's talking about it. We don't have to say a word. Everywhere you've gone, Jesus Christ has become the subject of conversation. You've made Him the issue."

Dr. Ferris Whitesell once wrote: "The New Testament churches were nerve centers of evangelism and in this respect constitute a pattern for local churches everywhere."[2]

How long has it been since you sat down and read the Book of Acts straight through? What a fascinating account! You talk about a church on fire and growing! I went through the Book of Acts recently and pulled out some of the phrases that describe the spread of the gospel in those days. Feel the strong, steady pulse of the young church in these descriptive phrases: "filled Jerusalem" (5:28); "went everywhere" (8:4); "in all the cities" (8:40); "all who dwelt at Lydda and Sharon"

(9:35); "throughout all Joppa" (9:42); "throughout all the region" (13:49); "all who dwelt in Asia heard" (19:10); "throughout almost all Asia" (19:26).

You could call that *saturation evangelism.* It was like pouring water onto a thick sheet of paper and watching the moisture spread as the paper absorbs it—until it touches every corner. Jesus Christ was the subject wherever you went in that first-century world. His life, His words, His death, and resurrection dominated conversations. People were coming to Christ by the thousands, being discipled, worshiping together, and winning still more and more people.

What was going on during this period of seven years? It began with the Lord Jesus Christ and twelve guys—one who didn't pass the course. And because they believed their main purpose in life was not to raise money or build buildings or sell books or influence public policy or argue over prophecy, but to share Jesus Christ, their faith and joy sent shock waves throughout the world.

The last command of our Lord was His first concern: to go into all the world and declare His salvation, purchased on the cross.

I don't think God wants everybody to go to Africa or India. Maybe not even to Haiti or Mexico or Utah. But God wants all people to go somewhere—to their business places, to their neighbors, to their children, to their communities. He has commanded all of us to have a heart and a passion for evangelism. We may not win many, but we are always to be on the alert for opportunities to declare our faith.

Only one truth saves. Only one gospel brings eternal life. There is only one escape from hell. We need to go to men and women and children with the precious gospel of Jesus Christ and declare His love for them. The same gospel that worked in your parents' generation will work today because, as Paul put it, "it is the power of God unto salvation." It is eternally relevant. It still changes lives.

Paul's words to the Ephesians take us all to task: "Be very careful, then, how you live—not as unwise but as wise, making the most of every opportunity, because the days are evil" (Ephesians 5:15–16 NIV).

Now, I'm not talking about buttonholing people or being obnoxious. That's not what we are to do. I'm just talking about beginning each day by praying,

"Lord, today I want to live for You. And Lord, if You bring someone across my path today who needs You, help me to sense it. And help me to do the right thing."

Andrew went to find his brother Peter and said, "I have someone I can't wait for you to meet. Come with me." And he brought his brother to Jesus.

It was just that simple.

It still is.

Chapter 4
Edifying One Another Matters

T HE END OF THE TWENTIETH CENTURY
brought a demolition ball swinging around in
America, and walls fell all around us. It was a time
of scandal, denials, recriminations, brazen defiance,
and national shame. People at the very pinnacle of
national leadership seemed determined to tear down
everything important to our country's future.

We tore down integrity, truth, purity, honesty,
and respect. We demolished the very things many of
us longed to rebuild in our nation. Not since the
Vietnam War had our population been so divided
and embittered. From talk radio to letters to the
newspaper to the very halls of Congress, Americans
seemed intent on putting their own spin on these
shameful events.

And we've torn one another down in the process!

But I want to write about something better—an alternative to this wholesale demolition. While we cannot stop the erosion and the tearing down of biblical values in our culture, we can do something about building one another up. In fact, we must!

BUILDING UP HIS PEOPLE

Leaping out of our Bible pages is a word that speaks to our mission as believers in a clear and specific way. It's the word *edification*. You may have heard it tossed around, if you've spent much time in evangelical circles. It's one of those spiritual-sounding terms we sometimes hear in church. It certainly sounds impressive, but what does it really mean?

Actually, it's pretty simple. The Greek term means to "build the house." That's it. That's all. Build the house.

Jesus used the term literally in Matthew 7:24 when He said, "Therefore whoever hears these sayings of Mine, and does them, I will liken him to a wise man who *built his house* on the rock" (emphasis added).

We get excited about building buildings and seeing them take shape. The New Testament, however, is much more concerned about building *people*. Most often in Scripture, *edify* is used in a metaphorical sense to mean "building up one another." Build up the body of Christ. Build up fellow believers. That, I believe, is what you and I are to be about until Jesus comes again.

It's a sad story, but I have met scores of people here at our church who say, "Please don't ask me to do anything. Just let me come and heal for a while. You can't believe how I was torn down at our last church. I need time to be *built back up.*"

When a church doesn't function according to the pattern of the Word of God, it can be one of the most destructive places anywhere. How that must grieve the heart of the Master Builder!

One of the most important statements from the lips of our Savior is this, found in Matthew 16:18: He said, "I will build My church, and the gates of Hades shall not prevail against it." Was Jesus talking about some brick-and-stone structure with a steeple on top? No, He was talking about the worldwide body of believers.

The church is built up externally through evangelism. God adds people to the body as we baptize them, and they become part of the church. But the church is built up internally through edification, through how we strengthen, encourage, and minister to one another in the body of Christ.

Let's face it: When you walk out into the world, you walk into an environment that automatically tears you down. Christians are no longer viewed with favor by our culture. Our beliefs and concerns are under attack in the schools, in the universities, in the entertainment industry, and in the mainstream media. It's hostile out there! We can get beaten up just going about our business.

We gather with our brothers and sisters to get built back up, so we can go back into the world and face the challenges again. That process has to be an intentional goal of every one of us, or we will be victimized by our culture.

In another world picture, Scripture refers to believers as "living stones" in a building being constructed by the Lord. Peter writes, "You also, as living stones [that's you and me], are being built up a spiritual house, a

holy priesthood, to offer up spiritual sacrifices accept-
able to God through Jesus Christ" (1 Peter 2:5). We *are*
the building—a living entity that spans culture and
language, heaven and earth, time and eternity.

The real church is not the building: It's people!
Redeemed men and women. If you moved your
whole congregation out to the parking lot on
Sunday, the church wouldn't be *in the building* any-
more. The church would be out in the parking lot.
Paul said as much to the Corinthians: "For we are
God's fellow workers; you are God's field, you are
God's building" (1 Corinthians 3:9).

What Is Edification All About?

When you survey the word *edification* through
Scripture, it's amazing the things you can learn.

It's not about you; it's about the saints. You and I
are called to build up and strengthen one another.
I'm called to build you up. You're called to build me
up. I must be very careful not to tear you down by my
actions, inaction, or words.

I heard about a young preacher who began one of

his messages by asking his congregation for honest feedback. "I want to get better at this," he told them. "And when I am finished, I hope you'll tell me how I'm doing."

Now, it's a risky thing to open yourself up like that, because there are those (for whatever reason) who take perverse delight in being hypercritical. Such was the case with an older gentleman who approached the young man afterward.

"The first thing I need to tell you," he said, "is you stunk!"

"Oh, my word!" said the pastor. "That's terrible! Can you be more specific? Can you help me a little here?"

The old man was more than happy to comply. "I'll give you three things," he sniffed. "Number one: You read your sermon. Number two: You read it poorly. And number three: It wasn't worth reading in the first place."

That, my friend, is not building up. That crusty old man, who thought he knew so much, was evidently ignorant (or willfully ignorant) of Paul's words in Ephesians: "Do not let any unwholesome talk come out of your mouths, but only what is helpful for *building others up* according to their needs, that it may benefit those who listen" (4:29 NIV, emphasis added).

You never forget critical remarks like that. They tend to replay in your head during times of discouragement. You and I can become so adept at tearing down, can't we? We're demolition experts. We know just where to swing the hammer and apply the crowbar. Yet, tearing down is the polar opposite of our calling in Scripture.

You say, "Where do you get that principle?" Please take a close look at these verses: "All things are lawful for me, but not all things are helpful; all things are lawful for me, but not all things *edify*. Let no one seek his own, but each one the other's wellbeing" (1 Corinthians 10:23–24).

Paul is saying, "There are many things I might do and many things I might say. But my first concern ought not to be me. My first thought ought to be, *Will this build up or tear down my brother or sister in the body?*

That's the emphasis in God's Word: Build the church! Don't get sidetracked into areas that benefit only you. Every word that leaves my mouth ought to be spoken with careful regard to those who will hear it. It's not about me; it's about the saints.

It's not what you profess; it's what you pursue. People-building is something you have to work at. It isn't always easy. It takes thought and discipline. I'm amazed at how quickly I can slip into a spirit of sarcasm or cynicism (especially when I'm tired) with my staff at church or at home with my family. I've been asking the Lord to rid me of that tendency.

Truthfully, I cannot think of any good use for sarcasm. Sometimes when you're in a comfortable environment with buddies and friends, you can get to tossing remarks back and forth—he zings you, you zing him right back, and it's all in "good fun," right?

Yet, you never know—sometimes people weigh your words, even words spoken in jest, much more heavily than you think they do. Maybe a month or two later you learn that some off-the-top remark you made stuck in someone's heart. You were "just kidding," but the remark pushed on a sore spot. It hurt. And that hurt may begin to fester.

It's easy to tear people down in a seemingly jest-ing, offhand way. It's something we do in our culture. If we don't feel secure in where we are, we think we can climb up on somebody else's failure. But the Bible tells us, "Therefore let us *pursue* the things which make for peace and the things by which one may *edify* another. Do not destroy the work of God" (Romans 14:19–20).

Did you see that? Let us *pursue* those things. Let's go after them. The *New International Version* says, "Let us therefore *make every effort* to do what leads to peace and to mutual edification." In other words, we have to do it intentionally. It won't happen accidentally. You don't get up one morning and float through the day edifying everyone you pass. You have to be on your knees before God, asking Him to fill you with His Spirit. You have to ask Him to show you opportunities to build others up. Then you have to do it!

It's not how much you know; it's how much you care. First Corinthians 8:1 says, "Knowledge puffs up, but *love builds up*" (NIV, emphasis added). Edification isn't about how smart you are. It's not about how many courses you have taken in school, how many seminary classes you have under your belt, or how many impressive books you've read. Edification starts primarily in the heart when you open your eyes, see people you care about, and find ways to love and encourage them.

When you've been wounded yourself, you begin to see wounded people in a new light. You find yourself with an entirely different attitude toward hurting people. My bouts with cancer have forever changed the way I view people in pain. And that's precisely what Paul said would happen in his second letter to the Corinthians: "Thank God, the Father of our Lord Jesus Christ, that he is our Father and the source of all mercy and comfort. For he gives us comfort in all our trials so that we in turn may be able to give the same sort of strong sympathy to others in their troubles that we receive from God. Indeed, experience shows that the more we share in Christ's immeasurable suffering the more we are able to give of his encouragement" (2 Corinthians 1:3–5 PHILLIPS).

Sharing the encouragement of Jesus has little to do with head knowledge and everything to do with the inclination of the heart.

It's not about your gifts; it's about your goals. I'm glad for the books and seminars and tests that help people identify their spiritual gifts. I believe everyone has a gift and ought to be aware of it and how to put it to work for the Lord. But once you have that nailed down, don't forget what the gift is for.

Some treat their spiritual gifts as my little grandson treated his soccer ball. He thought that ball was the center of his universe. Whenever he saw me, he said, "Ball," because I played ball with him whenever he was around. Whenever he looked through a magazine and saw something round, he said, "Ball." Once he saw a huge water tank in a Florida city, and he said, "Ball." Sometimes the boy had a one-track mind. Of course, his father and his grandfather knew he was just getting started toward an All-American career.

As he gets older, he's discovering that it's really hard to play soccer by yourself, and you really need someone with more skill than your grandfather. He's learning that soccer or baseball or football is a team game and that real joy comes in pursuing the goal of winning as a part of a team.

Unfortunately, some Christians never learn that
lesson about the Christian life. They view their spiritual gifts as if they were for their own use and enjoyment
alone. They don't seem to understand that the greatest
sense of fulfillment as believers is to see how God is
using their spiritual gifts to enhance the body of Christ
and build up a winning team for His honor and glory.

The apostle really takes off the gloves in two pas-
sages speaking to this matter. He leaves no doubt
where he stands. In 1 Corinthians 14:12, he says,
"Even so you, since you are zealous for spiritual gifts,
let it be for the edification of the church that you
seek to excel." That's pretty plain, isn't it? You don't
have to look that verse up in a commentary to understand what he means.

Later in the chapter he writes, "How is it then,
brethren? Whenever you come together, each of you
has a psalm, has a teaching, has a tongue, has a revelation, has an interpretation. Let all things be done
for edification" (1 Corinthians 14:26). Paul was saying, "When you get together, folks, don't be so con-
sumed with how you're going to exercise this or that
gift. It's not your gift that's important; it's your goal

with that gift. What are you doing with it? The gift itself ought to be incidental.

There is no time for self-centered preoccupation with gifting. In this hostile culture where believers get torn down just walking out their front doors, we need to pour all our energies into building up the body of Christ. It's all about the goal; it's not about the gift.

It's not about your wisdom; it's about His Word. How do we know where to start this important process? You may be asking yourself, *How am I going to turn this around? I know I've been negative. I know I say things I shouldn't and sometimes tear people down. I've done it for years. What can I do? Where do I learn to be a better builder?*

One of my favorite scenes in all the New Testament is Paul's encounter with the Ephesian elders on the beach at Miletus. Knowing he would never see these men again, he left them with this counsel: "So now, brethren, I commend you to God and to the word of His grace, which is able to build you up and give you an inheritance among all those who are sanctified" (Acts 20:32).

How do you get built up to the point that you can

build up somebody else? My friends, you need the
Book! Read the Bible. Study it. Memorize it. Meditate
on it. If you're not spending time in the Word of God,
I can almost promise that you will tear down your own
life and tend to tear down the lives of others in turn.
The Word of God is the fuel to help you be a builder.
That's how you build yourself up, so that you, in turn,
may build up the lives of others (see Jude 20–21).

Let's Please the Master Builder

We need one another. We need one another's strength,
help, encouragement, wisdom, warnings, and counsel.
The growing hostility of our culture and the wholesale
demolition of our nation's formerly godly foundations
ought to drive us together as never before.

Scripture says, "Edify"—build the house. And
while you're busy building in someone else's life,
you'll find your own life being repaired, restored,
and remodeled as well.

The Master Builder sees it all . . . and is well
pleased!

Chapter 5
Pursuing Your Reward Matters

WHEN OUR CHILDREN WERE LITTLE, we used to load the whole Jeremiah tribe into the station wagon every year for a family vacation. We always enjoyed family together times, but as young parents, Donna and I became distressed by the constant squabbles in the backseats.

"No, that's mine! You can't have it! Mom, make him leggo!"

"I got to sit by the window last time, and I'm gonna sit by the window this time too."

"He touched my elbow!"

"She breathed on me!"

After a while, those skirmishes began to steal some of the joy from our family excursions. Then my resourceful wife came up with an ingenious program. She called all the kids into the living room.

Then she pulled out some coins—rolls of quarters for the older kids and rolls of dimes for the younger ones. She handed out the booty to our children, who stared wide-eyed at their sudden wealth.

This, Donna explained to them, was their spending money for the entire vacation. But before they could let loose with a cheer, she added her one condition. She would retain the prerogative to retrieve money back from them—a coin at a time—when they did not behave as instructed in the car.

Of course the kids had to test the system. We hadn't gone very far before I heard her say to one of the younger ones, "Okay, you owe me a dime. Hand it over." So one dime returned (most reluctantly) to her purse. After that, it wasn't long before a few quarters started coming to the front seat.

And then, things began to change. At least two of the children radically changed their whole mentality about what they would say and do in the car. I had never heard those two so quiet and calm in my whole life. They turned a blind eye to offenses and refused to be provoked. They were determined to beat the system and keep that money!

Yes, the Jeremiah family found the secret to tranquillity in travel. It's called "rewards"!

Did you know that rewards are a major part of God's plan for His kids too? I know many people—godly people—who feel uncomfortable even discussing this issue. They reason, I suppose, that even thinking about future rewards displays a wrong or lesser motivation. We ought to work hard and stay pure and lay down our lives out of love for the Lord alone, they think.

But the Bible shows no such timidity. In fact, Scripture is filled with truth about rewards! And it speaks of them in the context of our motivations.

Bottom line, God rewards His servants. He is pleased and delighted to do so, and I believe a careful study of Scripture reveals that He wants us to be motivated by those promised rewards.

HEAVEN'S REWARD SYSTEM

Through the pages of this book, we have considered our Lord's final warnings—His words of hope and encouragement as we move through a new millennium. One of those wonderful challenges appears near the end of the Bible's final book. The Lord Jesus says, "Behold, I am coming quickly, and My reward is with Me, to give to every one according to his work" (Revelation 22:12).

In this study, we've heard our Lord Jesus describe the things that matter to Him as we await His return. He has told us that doing His business matters. Evangelizing and edifying matter. God in no way wants His people sitting around, doing nothing until Christ returns. He wants us to be busy. And in order to energize us in the service of the King, He has put a system of rewards into place. We ought to carefully consider those rewards. In fact, it would please Him if we did.

As a young boy growing up in my father's church, I remember how Sunday school attendance awards used to be a big deal. Do you remember them? If you came to Sunday school so many weeks without missing, you got a pin to wear on your shirt or dress or jacket. And then every so often after that, you could win additional pins by hanging in there week after week.

You could look around the church and see those

things gleaming on people's clothing. Some of those chains of pins got so long you began to wonder if someone would trip over them on the way to church. I remember people who really got into the display mode, parading their medals like a retired Russian general.

I'm sure there must have been Sundays when they felt lousy and didn't want to go to church, but hey, when you've got a five-and-a-half-year string going, you don't want to wimp out just because you're sick.

The rewards of heaven, however, go infinitely beyond stickpins or rolls of quarters and dimes. In fact, even though we might list Bible verses by the score, we can never really understand in this life how wonderful and desirable those heavenly rewards will be. As Paul wrote, "No eye has seen, no ear has heard, no mind has conceived what God has prepared for those who love him" (1 Corinthians 2:9 NIV, emphasis added).

Even so, it is good for us to focus on these verses. Listen to some of these biblical statements that describe God's system of rewards.

And men will say, "Surely there is a reward for the righteous; surely there is a God who judges on earth!" (Psalm 58:11 NASB)

You, O Lord, are loving. Surely you will reward each person according to what he has done. (Psalm 62:12 NIV)

Jesus said, "For whoever gives you a cup of water to drink in My name, because you belong to Christ, assuredly, I say to you, he will by no means lose his reward." (Mark 9:41)

Rejoice and be exceedingly glad, for great is your reward in heaven, for so they persecuted the prophets who were before you. (Matthew 5:12)

You just can't read the Bible without bumping into rewards. Of course, it doesn't mean something *owed* to us. It doesn't mean fair wages. It doesn't mean you get paid ten dollars an hour for a job that's worth ten dollars an hour. No, it's more like winning the Publisher's Clearing House ten-million-dollar

sweepstakes! Does the winner ever *earn* that money?
No. But does he have to qualify to receive it? Yes.
Does he have to follow the rules and do what the
instructions tell him to do in order to win? Yes. Does
filling out the forms and sending them in on time
earn the winner his money? Has he done enough
work to be owed all that money? Clearly, no. But
what he did qualified him for the prize, a prize hugely
out of proportion to the labor he expended.

That's what the Bible means by rewards.

The New Testament speaks of a very well-defined
system; after the rapture of the church, God will
reward His people. One of the first events that will
take place in heaven after the Rapture is the judgment
seat of Christ, or the *bema*, where all believers will
stand before the Lord. This will not be to determine
where we will spend eternity. That subject won't even
come up, because it will have already been decided.
At the *bema*, you and I will stand before our Lord and
be judged with a view to rewards.

The Bible tells us that after the church is taken to
heaven, either by rapture or by the resurrection, individual believers will be judged for their works done

in the body as Christians. At that time, special rewards will be handed out.

Who is going to stand before the judgment seat of Christ? A brother. A Christian. The *bema* is not for nonbelievers.

In 2 Corinthians 5:10 we read, "For we must all appear before the judgment seat of Christ, that each one may receive what is due him for the things done in the body, whether good or bad" (NIV).

In 1 Corinthians chapter 3, which is the central passage on this truth, we read these amazing words:

> For no other foundation can anyone lay than that which is laid, which is Jesus Christ. Now if anyone builds on this foundation with gold, silver, precious stones, wood, hay, straw, each one's work will become clear; for the Day will declare it, because it will be revealed by fire; and the fire will test each one's work, of what sort it is. If anyone's work which he has built on it endures, he will receive a reward. If anyone's work is burned, he will suffer loss; but he himself will be saved, yet so as through fire. (vv. 11–15, emphasis added)

Now let me set the stage a little. The Bible tells us there will be two major judgments in the future. The first is the one we just looked at, the judgment seat of Christ. This takes place in heaven during the time of the Tribulation on earth, immediately following the Rapture.

Then, after the thousand-year reign of Christ upon the earth is complete, there will be the judgment at the Great White Throne. At that time (terrible to contemplate!) nonbelievers will be judged for their sin and their rejection of God's grace and salvation in Christ.

Don't confuse these two events! Not a single nonbeliever will stand before the judgment seat of Christ. The judgment of nonbelievers will be reserved for the Great White Throne later on.

This Is *Not* About Judgment of the Believer's Sin

Let me tell you why I know that. The Bible tells us that judgment already took place. It's over! When was your sin judged? It was judged at the cross of

Jesus Christ. Your sins will not be judged, because God already poured out the full fury of His judgment and wrath on Jesus Christ as He hung there on the cross, between heaven and earth, on our behalf.

Christ was condemned for us. Galatians 1:3–4 tells us that "our Lord Jesus Christ . . . gave Himself for our sins, that He might deliver us from this present evil age." Romans 8:1 says, "There is therefore now no condemnation to those who are in Christ Jesus." You will never face your sin again.

People ask me, "But Pastor Jeremiah, how can someone have his sins forgiven and still have his works reviewed at the judgment seat of Christ? Don't those ideas seem to be in conflict?"

No, because forgiveness is about justification, and rewards are about the things we do as justified people. These are not works done for justification; they are works done as a justified person.

One of the greatest truths about Scripture that I have learned through the years is the concept of biblical tension. God has put the Word together in such a way that if we read it carefully, we will not veer off to the left or the right, to this extreme or that extreme. For instance, one of the great truths about a Christian is that we are saved by faith, not by works. Ephesians 2:8–9 says, "For by grace you have been saved through faith, and that not of yourselves; it is the gift of God, not of works, lest anyone should boast."

Now, most people stop right there. But the passage goes on: "For we are His workmanship, created in Christ Jesus for good works, which God prepared beforehand that we should walk in them" (v. 10).

Do you see that? What Paul said to the Ephesians was this: "You can't do enough works to get saved. But when you become a Christian, it is apparent that the very purpose for which God has saved you is so that you might live your life as an open testimony and do good works for His glory."

The issue before the judgment seat of Christ will be the works we have done after salvation. Someday you are going to stand before the mighty Son of God "whose eyes are like blazing fire" (Revelation 2:18 NIV), and He will walk you through a review of your life as a believer. And the issue at that time will be rewards.

THIS IS *NOT* ABOUT ONE BELIEVER'S JUDGMENT OF ANOTHER BELIEVER

We're quick to judge. Some people regard it as a favorite indoor sport. Yet we ought to constantly remind ourselves that God has not called any of us to judge anyone else. Because all believers must stand before the judgment seat of Christ, every one of us giving account of himself to God, we have no right to judge the work or the motives of other believers.

When it comes right down to it, you really don't know my motives, do you? Nor do I know yours. You can't see my heart of hearts, and I can't see yours. We may form our opinions along the way, but I can promise you this: There will be a great many surprises at the judgment seat of Christ. You can count on it!

First Corinthians 4:5 offers a timely warning: "Therefore judge nothing before the appointed time; wait till the Lord comes. He will bring to light what is hidden in darkness and will expose the motives of men's hearts. At that time each will receive his praise from God" (NIV).

What a great reminder that it is not our job to judge others. The Lord says, "You leave that to Me."

Five Crowns

Let's take a few moments to survey five of the rewards mentioned in the New Testament.

1. *The Crown of the Victor.* In 1 Corinthians 9:25–27, Paul writes, "Everyone who competes in the games goes into strict training. They do it to get a crown that will not last; but we do it to get a crown that will last forever" (NIV). The apostle speaks here about an imperishable crown, a crown that will last forever. "This," says Paul, "is the crown I'm going after." He uses a word picture that would have been very compelling to that particular group of believers. The Corinthians had two great athletic events in their time, the Olympic Games and the Isthmian Games. The Isthmian Games were held in Corinth. So this would have been like Paul writing to New Yorkers and making reference to the Yankees team — or talking to Green Bay folks about their Packers. Paul had their attention!

Contestants in those games had to rigorously train for ten months. The last month was spent in Corinth, where contestants were supervised daily in the gymnasium and on the athletic fields. The race was always a major attraction at the games; that is the figure Paul used to illustrate the faithful Christian life. Many may run in this race, he said, but only one receives the prize. No one would train so hard and so long without intending to win. Yet out of the large number of runners in the Isthmian Games, only one would win.

The Isthmian athletes worked diligently for a long time to gain an insignificant prize. Paul's thought was, "How much more should we as Christians take control of our bodies, take control of our energies, take control of our motives and our purposes, and discipline ourselves so that we can be useful servants of God!" The man or woman who does that is a candidate for the imperishable crown, the victor's crown.

At the *bema* seat of Christ, earthly wreaths and trophies and newspaper clippings and Super Bowl rings will be long forgotten. They'll be no more important than brushing your teeth or buying a newspaper at the corner store. But what we do for eternity—even the smallest of deeds—will count forever.

You and I have a chance to win this victor's crown, and it is infinitely worth the effort. When we make the choice to put God first, no matter what, when we use our energies for His purposes, we are reaching for that beautiful crown.

2. *The Crown of Rejoicing.* This second reward has been called the soul winner's crown. First Thessalonians 2:19 tells us, "For what is our hope, or joy, or crown of rejoicing? Is it not even you in the presence of our Lord Jesus Christ at His coming?"

There will be a crown given to those who take a lot of people to heaven with them. Through the years I have met a number of individuals who never ceased winning people to Jesus Christ. It was their passion, their delight, their reason for getting up in the morning. And when we meet these people in heaven someday, we will know them by this radiant crown of rejoicing. And who wouldn't rejoice as you look around heaven and see men and women and children whom you had the privilege of introducing to the Savior? These are the ones who will welcome you "into eternal dwellings" (Luke 16:9 NIV).

3. *The Crown of Righteousness.* "Finally, there is laid up for me the crown of righteousness, which the Lord, the righteous Judge, will give to me on that Day, and not to me only but also to all who have loved His appearing" (2 Timothy 4:8). There will be a crown given to those who look forward to our Lord's return. Frankly, I don't see many people doing that these days. It isn't fashionable or chic to talk about the Second Coming. When I was a boy, I remember how people used to say to one another, "It may be today!" or "Maybe tonight." So many these days are caught up in the details of the present age: politics, the stock market, making money, and recreating on the weekends. We aren't longing for His return because we're too busy living life in the fast lane. Nevertheless, our Lord has reserved special recognition for those who watch and long for His return.

4. *The Crown of Life.* James 1:12 says, "Blessed is the man who endures temptation [testing]; for when he has been approved, he will receive the crown of life which the Lord has promised to those who love Him."

Believing men, women, and children often endure humiliation, deprivation, bitter persecution, and even death for their faith in the Lord Jesus. It's happening today in countries all over the world. These dear brothers and sisters will also stand before the judgment seat of Christ—and our Lord will not overlook their suffering. Each will be crowned with an unspeakably beautiful crown of life—the martyr's crown—because they paid for their faith with their very lives.

5. *The Crown of Glory.* This final crown will be presented to faithful pastors and leaders. Peter wrote, "And when the Chief Shepherd appears, you will receive the crown of glory that does not fade away" (1 Peter 5:4). There is a unique crown for those who faithfully teach the Word of God and shepherd God's people—an activity so near and dear to the Great Shepherd's heart. If we are steadfast in pouring out our lives for those under our care, God will provide us with an unfading, eternal crown.

THE LORD HIMSELF IS YOUR CHIEF REWARD

As Abraham returned from defeating the pagan kings, he was met by the grateful king of Sodom, who sought to reward the patriarch. Abraham stead-fastly refused, telling this godless ruler, "I have raised my hand to the LORD, God Most High, the Possessor of heaven and earth, that I will take nothing, from a thread to a sandal strap, and that I will not take any-thing that is yours, lest you should say, 'I have made Abram rich'" (Genesis 14:22–23).

Abraham was saying, "Man, I don't want so much as a shoelace. Keep the stuff yourself." Then, in the very next verse after Abraham's reply, the Lord appears to him and says, "Do not be afraid, Abram. I am your shield, your exceedingly great reward" (Genesis 15:1).

In other words, "You made the right choice, son. You rejected the earthly king's booty, and now I, the King of the universe, will reward you with everything that I am."

We may not be enriched or rewarded or acknowl-edged for our efforts through the days of our lives. But oh my friend, a day is coming! The Lord who misses nothing will reward us with the beauty and glory and nearness of His presence through endless ages. There can be no better reward than God Himself.

Pursue your reward till He comes, my friend. I can't even describe how much is at stake. This is no time to be idle or to allow ourselves to be caught up in peripheral matters that sap our energy and strength and desire.

Let's live for heaven, remembering that He could come with the next heartbeat . . . and remembering that the smile of His favor is worth everything, infinitely more than earth's best treasures.

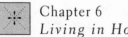

Chapter 6
Living in Hope Matters

A FEW YEARS AGO I read an article that cited an example given by Major F. J. Harold Cushner, an army medical officer during the Vietnam War, who was held prisoner by the Vietcong for five and a half years. He told *New York Magazine* about meeting a twenty-four-year-old marine, who had already survived two years of prison camp.

The marine seemed to be in relatively good health and appeared to be doing fine. When Cushner asked him how he happened to be doing so well, the young man explained that the camp commander had promised him an early release if he cooperated in every respect. Because the marine had seen other prisoners granted such a gift, he agreed. He became a model prisoner and served as head of the camp's "thought reform group," which tried to brainwash other prisoners.

As time passed, however, it became clear to the marine that his captors had lied to him. When this realization finally hit home, the young man became a zombie. He refused all work and rejected all offers of food and encouragement. He simply lay on his cot, sucking his thumb, until a few days later he died. When his hope of release vanished, he found he had nothing left to live for.[1]

Hope. Who among us can live without it?

JESUS AND HOPE

Our world has never needed hope more than it does today. Just as Jesus prophesied so long ago, we see kingdom rising against kingdom and ethnic group against ethnic group. Scores of old Soviet nuclear weapons have vanished, droughts and floods and earthquakes ravage the planet, scandals in government and business rock the nations, and we struggle with a world-wide recession. The ozone layer continues to shrink

while weapons of mass destruction continue to pro-
liferate.

Because our world looks like this, Mike Bellah,
in his article titled "Make Room for Baby Boomers,"
has written, this:

> Baby boomers desperately need hope. The church
> that reaches this generation will be one where hope
> is frequently dispensed. However, it is important that
> the church offer real, not contrived, hope. The kind
> of hope promised by the success gospel is looked on
> with a deserved cynicism by most baby boomers.
> Similarly, the hope offered by sincere but unrealistic
> Christians, which ignores real pain and suffering,
> will not help disillusioned baby boomers. This gen-
> eration will not respond to religious platitudes and
> clichés that minimize the hurt found in a fallen
> world. The church that offers hope to baby boomers
> will proclaim the God of Joseph, Daniel, Elijah and
> others like them. It will reveal a God who does not
> always remove us from our crises, but who supports
> us in them and brings us through them.[2]

Friend, we need some solid *hope!*

And, Jesus Christ *is* that hope!

The Lord's powerful ministry of hope was prophesied long before He walked this earth. The prophet Isaiah gloried in the storehouses of hope to be thrown open by the coming Messiah: "Those who hope in me will not be disappointed," he reports the Lord saying (Isaiah 49:23 NIV).

In his gospel, Matthew pointed to this prophetic emphasis on the hope Messiah was to bring. He tells us that the Lord "healed all their sick, warning them not to tell who he was," then adds this:

This was to fulfill what was spoken through the prophet Isaiah: "Here is my servant whom I have chosen, the one I love, in whom I delight; I will put my Spirit on him, and he will proclaim justice to the nations. He will not quarrel or cry out; no one will hear his voice in the streets. A bruised reed he will not break, and a smoldering wick he will not snuff out, till he leads justice to victory. In his name the nations will put their hope." (Matthew 12:15–21 NIV, quoting Isaiah 42:1–4)

This was the message the disciples needed to hear in the anxious days leading up to the Crucifixion. And they especially needed to remember it in the crushing days immediately following the death of our Lord. "You now have sorrow," Jesus had told them, "but I will see you again and your heart will rejoice, and your joy no one will take from you" (John 16:22).

We often feel as if we have been abandoned at the corner of Hopelessness and Despair. The good news is that we who know God through His Son, Jesus Christ, don't have to be left at such a desperate corner. There is an answer, and His name is Jesus.

That's not trite. It's not merely theological. It's not just church talk. It's true.

PETER AND HOPE

In 1 Peter chapter 1, the apostle makes an important statement about the nature of our hope. Peter knew how important it was to dispense such hope to his readers. He knew the recipients of his little letter were enduring tremendous hardships.

These Christians, salted throughout the Roman Empire, lived at a time when Rome tyrannized believers. They faced untold persecution and suffering.

Peter has a good word for us about how to face troubled times. That word is hope. He insists we can live in hope if we understand and believe the truth concerning the risen Christ. In 1 Peter 1:3 he says, "Blessed be the God and Father of our Lord Jesus Christ, who according to His abundant mercy has begotten us again to a living hope through the resurrection of Jesus Christ from the dead."

A living hope.

Peter would have us believe that the hope we seek and that so often seems to elude us (if we don't carefully listen to God's Word) is to be found in the Person who has overcome death.

I Remember When . . .

I wonder what was going through Peter's mind as he wrote these words. I can't help but think that when the apostle proclaimed a living hope in the resurrected Christ, his own personal experience rushed back into his mind in Technicolor and surround-sound.

Peter had been a very close friend of the Lord. He had walked with Him through most of His public ministry. Oh, it's true he'd had some problems. He denied the Lord and had to be recommissioned. That's why we all like Peter so much; he gives us a sense of identity. We believe that if he could make it with the Lord, maybe we can too. But in the end, Peter loved the Lord and hoped that this Jesus was the One who would be their Messiah, who would free them from Roman bondage. Peter was like all the rest who had pinned their hope on Jesus.

Then one day it happened: the anger, the accusations, the mock trial, the beating, the crown of thorns, the cross, the journey up the hill, the nails, the spear, the darkness. And everything Peter had believed in, everything he had hoped for, was taken down from that cross, wrapped in linen, and laid in a cold, rock-hewn tomb.

If we could have looked into Peter's heart during the days between the death of Christ and His resurrection, I think we would have seen the epitome of hopelessness and despair. The Gospels make it clear that Peter was dumbfounded by what was happening. Shell-shocked.

Then on the third day, word started to filter down that friends had visited the tomb, looked inside — and found it empty. Had the body been stolen? But Peter was from Missouri. "Show me," he demanded. He wanted to see for himself. He ran to the tomb with John and when he stooped, looked in, and saw the Lord's garments by themselves, Scripture says the reality of the resurrection of Jesus Christ began to dawn in his heart.

And then came the moment when he saw the resurrected Lord Himself. He examined the nail prints in His hands and the place where the spear had pierced His side. It overwhelmed Peter to realize that this One whom he had seen die, go into the grave, and remain there for three days, had on the third day exploded from the tomb by His own power, victorious over man's greatest enemy. Jesus had come back from the dead. He was alive! He was the risen Lord!

So Peter wrote to his friends who were suffering, "I want to tell you something. You have a living hope, a hope based upon what Jesus Christ did when He arose from the grave. You see, He defeated the greatest enemy that man faces. He, by Himself, gained victory over death—and He promises that those who put their faith in Him shall also overcome death."

Are you looking for hope in difficult times? Are you trying to sort out the circumstances of your life? If so, look to Christ, because that is where hope is to be found.

Peter says it's found in the person of the Lord Jesus Christ. We pin our hope on Him because He is the only One who ever did what He did. He came out of death alive, victorious over the grave, and He promises us that if we put our trust in Him, even as He lives, we, too, shall live. There is hope in Christ Jesus! No matter how dark our situation might become, our hope is anchored in Jesus Christ and in His power over death.

The reality of this came home to me recently when I read an article written by Joni Eareckson Tada. Joni is no stranger to tragedy and difficulty. Paralyzed in a diving accident at age seventeen, she has since ministered to millions across the world with the message of hope in Christ.

In an article she told about saying to her assistant one day, "File this, Francie, and make copies of this letter, would you? And, oh, yes, would you please pull out the sofa bed one more time?" Her paralysis blocks her body from feeling pain, and the only way she knows something is wrong is when her temperature and blood pressure begin to rise. She intuitively senses something is wrong. Oftentimes it's because she has unknowingly punctured her body or has rubbed against something and suffered a bruise or laceration. Sometimes she has to ask her assistant to undress her and examine her body to see what's wrong.

In the article Joni said she was in the midst of one of these episodes—they happen three or four times a month—and looked up to the ceiling and said aloud, "I want to quit this. Where do I go to resign from this stupid paralysis?"

As Francie was leaving the office that day she ducked out the door, then stuck her head back in and said, "I bet you can't wait for the Resurrection."

Joni wrote, "My eyes dampened again, but this

time they were tears of relief and hope. I squeezed back my tears and dreamed what I've dreamed of a thousand times—the promise of the Resurrection. A flood of other hopeful promises filled my mind. When we see him we shall be like him. . . . The perishable shall put on the imperishable. . . . The corruptible, that which is incorruptible . . . That which is sown in weakness will be raised in power. . . . He has given us an inheritance that can never perish, spoil, or fade. I opened my eyes and said out loud with a smile, 'Come quickly, Lord Jesus.'" [3]

This hope of ours isn't merely "pie in the sky in the great by and by." It isn't merely a childish wish that we paint out in the far-flung future. It isn't merely that if we believe hard enough, things will get better. This is not *hope-so* hope; this is *know-so* hope. This is knowing the Person Who has done what no one else has ever done.

By virtue of that accomplishment, Jesus has laid claim to our faith and says, "If I came out of the grave victorious over death, and you put your trust in Me, you can have that same victory—not only over death, but in your life, day by day."

A Sure Hope

How sure is our hope? Notice what 1 Peter 1:4 says. This hope is "incorruptible and undefiled and . . . Does not fade away, reserved in heaven for you." You know what? Those four traits are out of reach for anyone who places his or her hope in earthly things.

Have you ever noticed how disappointing placing your faith in human things can be? It's so easy to get wrapped up in things that can never truly reward our fondest hopes, rather than the things that really matter. Of course, I'm not for a moment suggesting that we shouldn't put our hope and trust in one another, that we should not bond strongly with our families. But there is a hope beyond that—and more important than that! That is the hope we place in the eternal God through His Son, Jesus Christ.

Peter says such a hope won't die. It won't decay, deteriorate, or be destroyed. That hope is there for you in the person of Jesus Christ; and because He is eternal, your hope in Him is eternal.

That's why there is such a distinctiveness to the

way faithful Christian people respond to life. That's why they can handle the challenges that come their way. They may reel from the pressure, but down deep inside lies the quiet confidence that this, too, shall pass—and if it doesn't, it just gets better!

But What about Now?

You say, "Pastor Jeremiah, that's all well and good, and I'm glad about the future. That's going to be wonderful someday when we see the Lord and our hope is realized in an intimate, personal fellowship with Him. But I have to face next week. I get up in the morning and commute to a job that's terrorizing me. I have to live in a home situation that has me frantic. I have to deal with a disease that we can't control. How is my relationship with Jesus Christ going to make any difference in my life now? How does my hope about the future and eternity with Him affect the way I live today?"

Peter must have been anticipating that question, because he says that we who have placed our hope in Christ are "kept by the power of God through faith

for salvation ready to be revealed in the last time"
(1 Peter 1:5).

Now watch carefully. Here is how all the themes
in this chapter work together. First of all, Peter says
God has given us a hope that is secure, steadfast, and
that can never be touched. It is beyond decay or
destruction. Nothing can happen to it.

Second, in the very next verse Peter says God is
committed to helping us fully realize that hope. God
promises us a secure hope for our personal and eternal walk with Him and a day-by-day guarantee that
He will keep us through the process of experiencing
that hope. In fact, the word translated "kept" is one
of the strongest terms in the New Testament. It literally means "to be garrisoned about by an army."

In other words, Peter says, "Here you are with
your hope in Christ. You have fixed your eyes upon
Him. You believe He came out of the grave, you
trusted Him, and you believe that someday you, too,
will live for eternity. But all the way along as you
walk with Him, He has promised to keep you and to
help you every day."

It's no wonder that many have written about the

relationship between our eternal hope and our day-by-day experience of problems and difficulties. C. S. Lewis once said it this way: "Aim at Heaven and you will get earth 'thrown in': aim at earth and you will get neither."[4] That is a powerful truth. He means that if you don't choose the one and only path to heaven, you won't get there at all; and by missing heaven, you won't have anything worth living for down here either.

It's only as we fix our anchor in eternity that we find stability for life in these stress-filled days before our Lord's return. Oh, we'll still have problems. We're still in for a bumpy ride along the way. But there is a difference; our problems will finally begin to make sense if we pay attention to the things that matter and continue to live in hope.

Sooner or later in all of our lives we come to a fork in the road where we have to make a choice. Either we go on putting our trust in our own strength and in that which others may offer us in the human realm, or we choose the other realm and make our journey toward God. Hope in God is a decision we make. It is something that we choose.

Jesus is coming! He will come back for His own, and we will see Him face to face. And until that time, the Son of God lives within us and has promised to walk with us and never forsake us.

He lives! Hope is alive!

Because He Lives

One of my favorite people is Bill Gaither. He and his wife, Gloria, have given us much of the modern hymnody that we enjoy. It's a great heritage.

Bill tells how back in the early sixties, he and Gloria were going through some terribly difficult days. He had just endured a bout with mononucleosis; Gloria was suffering with mild depression; they were about to have a child. Gloria looked around at a world that seemed in utter turmoil and her heart filled with despair. Here this child was coming into their home and she thought, What kind of people are we to bring a child into this messed-up world?

One day she was in her study, quiet and waiting before the Lord, and the Spirit of God began to move upon her heart. He impressed upon her this central message of hope in Jesus Christ. He began to help her understand that life always conquers death—as long as that life is in Christ. Soon she began to grasp that life would conquer death, not just someday, but now. She saw that if we place our faith in the living Christ, we can conquer feelings of discouragement and depression prompted by the challenges of everyday life. She was so overcome by this realization that she tried to express it in the lyrics of a song, a hymn that has become very precious to us all. It goes like this:

Because He lives I can face tomorrow.
Because He lives all fear is gone.
Because I know He holds the future
And life is worth the living just because He lives.

And now you also know why she wrote the second verse of that song:

How sweet to hold our newborn baby,
And feel the pride and joy he gives.
But greater still the calm assurance
Our child can face uncertain days because He lives.

One day, not long after the song was written, Bill's father visited the Gaithers in Alexandria. He came into the office building where Gloria was working and said, "Hey, get Bill and come out here. I've got something to show you."

Just a few weeks before his visit, the parking lot at the building had been resurfaced. Workers had brought in stone, laid it down, and rolled it out with heavy machinery. Then they came in with pea gravel, also rolling it out. Next they covered the stone and gravel with hot, molten asphalt, rolled it, then finished by putting down and rolling another layer of asphalt.

Bill's father pointed to the middle of the parking lot and said, "Look at that!" Sure enough, right up through the rock, right up through the pea gravel, right up through the first layer of asphalt and right up through the second, had grown a tender, green shoot. It wasn't huge or substantial. A child could have reached down and plucked it out. But the shoot didn't come up because it was strong or sharp or because it had any special ability. It came up through that stone and gravel and asphalt because it had one quality: life. Life always reigns over no life![5]

Jesus Christ speaks to all of us today as we seek the hope we need for stable, positive, productive lives. Even in these tumultuous times, He reaches out to us and says, "Listen! I am the living God. I overcame death. I want to live within you and give you the hope you need to face the challenges of life."

If you have never put your hope in God through faith in His Son, Jesus Christ, you need to make that decision. That is where life begins! You can run to all kinds of psychological remedies for the hopelessness in your life, but if you do not know the risen Christ, you cannot find or enjoy ultimate hope . . . and you will continue to live at the corner of Hopelessness and Despair.

Whatever your circumstances today, whatever the weather, whatever situations press in on you, step out into the bright, warm sunlight of a hope that is alive. It is alive because He is alive, and it will never die because He lives forever.

When He comes, will Jesus find you doing the things that really matter to Him? Or will you, instead, just be doing what matter to you? Will you be busy doing the Lord's business when He comes? Will you be evangelizing the lost and edifying the saved? Will you be pursuing your heavenly reward with all your heart and living in the secure hope that He is coming again?

Never forget, Christian, before this day is over, before the sun sets over the hills, before you scratch another day off your calendar, He may call us all to Himself. In the twinkling of an eye, you will find yourself wrapped in the strong arms of Hope Himself.

Maybe today!

Endnotes

CHAPTER 3

1. Charles Panati, Panati's *Extraordinary Endings of Practically Everything and Everybody* (New York: Harper & Row, 1989), 398.
2. Ferris Daniel Whitesell, *Basic New Testament Evangelism* (Grand Rapids, Mich.: Zondervan, 1949), 133.

CHAPTER 4

1. Patrick M. Morley, "Building Our Kids," in *God's Vitamin "C" for the Spirit of Men*, comp. D. Larry Miller (Lancaster, Penn.: Starburst Publishers, 1996), 81.

CHAPTER 5

1. Robin Jones, retold by Casandra Lindell, "A Parable of God's Perspective," *More Stories for the Heart*, comp. Alice Gray (Sisters, Ore.: Multnomah, 1997), 270–71.

CHAPTER 6

1. Douglas Cooligan, "That Helpless Feeling: The Dangers of Stress," *New York Magazine*, 14 July 1975, 28.
2. Mike Bellah, "Make Room for Baby Boomers," *The Evangelical Beacon*, April 1991, 7.
3. Joni Eareckson Tada, "We Will Be Whole," *Today's Christian Woman*, March/April 1991, 35.
4. C. S. Lewis, *Mere Christianity* (New York: MacMillan, 1966), 118.
5. Gloria Gaither, *Because He Lives* (Grand Rapids, Mich.: Zondervan, 1997), 16, 21–22.